Morning Promises

&

My Evening Songs

To

By

Evelyn Dilworth-Williams

authorHOUSE™

1663 LIBERTY DRIVE, SUITE 200
BLOOMINGTON, INDIANA 47403
(800) 839-8640
WWW.AUTHORHOUSE.COM

First published by AuthorHouse 11/16/04

ISBN: 1-4208-0851-6 (sc)

Printed in the United States of America
Bloomington, Indiana

This book is printed on acid-free paper.

ACKNOWLEDGEMENTS

While this book of poetry, *Morning Promises & My Evening Songs*, is a reflection of my personal journey, I'm grateful to my loving family and wonderful friends for their encouragement and support, which was the catalyst that inspired me to share my poetic thoughts. I would like to thank my immediate family, especially my sons Chris and Jeff, for supporting the idea of this book. I am grateful to my entire church family (Sardis Missionary Baptist) for the positive responses I received when sharing my poetry with the congregation. Special thanks to my former co-worker, bowling teammate, and wonderful friend, Phyllis F. Jones, for sharing with me her writing expertise. Finally, I must thank my husband, Thomas, for supporting the idea of my verses and making comments that always inspired me to do more with my poems.

DEDICATIONS

In memory of my grandfathers,
Flenoy Little and Cleve Dilworth, Sr.,
the oldest visible mortal giants of my life.
They stood proud as time tested their existence,
I'm proud to be part of their lineage.
&
All the nonviolent Foot Soldiers of the 1960's Civil Rights
Revolution,
who honored the *promises* of our ancestors with deeds and *songs*.

Table of Contents

INTRODUCTION

Morning Promises & My Evening Songs

Gazing into the morning sunrise
Ne'er reveals how the day unfolds
A galactic wait for the sunset's tolls
To hear an evening's song surprise
All about a day's majesty of:
The Morning
To Midday
Then Evening
Followed by Night
Repeating Virgin Light
To guard secrets of the day
As the evening commands us to obey

Each phase of the day rewards us with blessings. Some are easily seen while others are disguised beyond understanding and still they are blessings. This book illustrates the moods of life during the course of a day (or life's moments in time) with the use of poetry and lyrics. The tune of each song is a personal experience of the person who's in need of that song. The book is divided into five sections:

Morning
Midday
Evening
Night
&
Morning Again

I will sing of mercy and judgment: unto thee,
O Lord, will I sing.

Psalm 101: 1

Every poem and song orders a change of heart an exchange for the betterment of tomorrow's start.

Evelyn Dilworth-Williams

M O R N I N G

Rising with hope to design a clean slated day

Evelyn Dilworth-Williams

Morning Promises

The dawning of the day is soft and tender
Feelings of renewal to make prior wrongs right
Awards the approach from the heavenly sender
Grabs the heart's mind with cerebral might

Rising with a brilliant premiere glare
With remnants of the life that's yours
Newly sworn energy to absorb despair
Embodying freshness of missed times before

The renewal of all of yesterday's passed task
Glistening with joyful hope that's sure to come
Knowing what lies ahead unveils life's mask
With virgin labor brightening a day's total sum

Sunrise pledges a better way
Creating time to make a blessed day
Knowing a certainty of rekindling will stay
The *morning promises* await the first sunray

Evelyn Dilworth-Williams

Power of Prayer

To start the day like the morning dew
Makes a day appear to create life anew
With a touch of softness and silent damp
The morning dew gives way to our daily lamp
To follow the gentle pattern of the day
Comes with the dew when we pray
Morning dew is our gift of cleansed peace
That emerges as long as prayer never ceases

The morning dew;
                    starts a day brand new

First Frost

Sunny days and starry nights
Moonlit sky embracing earth's sights
Denies vigilance from all that's of fright
Lacy crystals appear and limit life's delight

Bound by the appearance of a luminous existence
While life condenses the energy needed for resistance
Lacy crystals conjoin earth with heaven for coexistence
That makes the dawning of the sun void of distance

Still the first frost must appear
It's then the Savior draws us near
Even when laced with assigned fear
The first frost is surety of life's premiere

Evelyn Dilworth-Williams

Thank God for Sunday

All week long my soul is in fray
But on Sunday I'm ready to pray
Made it again to another day of rest
Seeking ways to be wondrously blessed

The Word is shouted and happily heard
Aiming at the spot in my heart that godly serves
Asking for forgiveness of all that I've done wrong
While praising and singing those old Zion songs

Moaning with the Saints about days that are past
Hoping the moment in time will forever hold fast
Thanking the Almighty for this time under grace
Wishing it'll sustain my week-long earthly pace

Feelings of rapture embrace my being
Carving new rank for my spirited-recovering
Grabbing hold of this moment in time
For fear of missing tomorrow's sunshine

Yet on this day I'll wash my spirit clean
This might be the day that I'm redeemed
My heart is full of worldly repentance
Sanctioning my life to a heavenly sentence

Though I stretch out my open hands
To receive Him and live by His plans
Another day I'm given another chance
Singing with angels and letting my soul dance

All the days that follow make my soul weary
Still I cleave until Sunday comes to bate the fury

All on the seventh day
When I congregate to kneel and pray

For it's the day I'm committed to rest
Seeking more ways to be wondrously blessed
Ne'er to worry about my life's challenges ahead
Sunday reassures me of His daily power instead

Evelyn Dilworth-Williams

Glorious Hope

The rising sun creates a day of glory
Shining so bright to reveal His story

Bringing forth rays of abundant hope
Making life's vision a worthy scope

Praising each ray as each ray beams,
Grateful for glory and blessed by its means

Much obliged and merciful as days unfold
The days of glory let me know what's untold

One of a Kind

Mother Nature nestles on tree leaves
Sharing all life's likeness in plain sight
Makes a distinguishable appearance
With children of earth-made might

Variety is the supernatural ordered day
While in search of the pious connection
Even the sun needs more than a daily spot
As differences emerge as solo perfection

Understand with appreciation
Life forms are not distorted variation
But a construct of divine manifestation
For we are not our bespoken creation

Not our sole creation: Repeat!!!
Not our own creation: Again repeat!!!
Not our personalized creation: Repeat!!!
Not our custom-made creation: Again repeat!!!

Uniquely made by an unmatched mind
Oh, what a creation!!!
Oh, what a creation!!!
A countless design that's one of a kind

Evelyn Dilworth-Williams

Gap

Trusting eyes

That can't always see

Make way for power

Coming from Thee

You are the Gap

Life's Map: Heaven's Home

Conceived with a map in hand
But ne'er visible to earthly man
Pertinent function to existence
To explore all of life's resistance
The home of each being is revealed
All entering have first love that's instilled
Important destinations are wisely chartered
Keeping life from becoming disheartened

First travels are vastly visible to the eye
Getting on the chartered course one can rely
Though travels through time stall offshore
Colliding with others' maps of times before
The early travels are the ones with ease
The dates fade quickly — no one is pleased
The hand disconnects from the map
And life's guides spin mishaps

The distance from our home at birth
To where we'll go traveling on earth
Intertwined in challenging man-made ways
Landing off course with a life of dismay
Where do we go without directions in life?
Do we make them up to avoid daily strife?
Or join others claiming the rules of travel?
Do we pretend to conquer life as it unravels?

Knowledge of the distance from birth to death
Travels fade along with the map's result of theft
Blinded conscious and going nowhere
In receipt of what's in life's despair
Going back home is often a difficult task

A return to the womb is where we'll find the map
Oftentimes given the chance to start anew
Or keep running aground we just continue

The final destination isn't achieved without a map
We just blunder around and going nowhere
Doing all sorts of things without human care
Making life's travel impossible to bear
An empty place awaits our arrival
Inhabiting it throughout eternity's survival
When all was needed was love of humankind
But die not reading the "Heaven's Home" sign

Love

A picnic on a rainy day
Detaches its splendor
With more promises
To recur again

Belief in its return
Keeps the soul sane
Reaching for more
Up-grading each day

Flawed perfection
Makes its claim
With the certainty
Of re-surfing time

Creating acceptance
With aging days
Attaching to the heart
A bond of belief

That a rainy day picnic
Keeps the plan alive
When the heart adjusts
For outcomes beyond

Evelyn Dilworth-Williams

Ms. Phyllis Wheatley?

I'm not feeling much like myself today
My pen writes such soft words
My voice seems to fade away
Wonder how I will be heard?

Could this be Ms. Wheatley
Writing and speaking soft words
Effectively and very sweetly
And as passionate as singing birds?

So many faces and spirits to bear
Wrenching my soul to an unknown
A gift received that I'll one day share
The giving of others and my very own

Could this be me writing so sweetly?
Voice and pen seem like a literary bouquet
Or is this the spirit of Ms. Wheatley?
I'm not feeling very much like myself today

Mess at the Gate

Someb'dy needs to set that child straight
Goin' to keep up mess all the way to hell's gate
Bothering everyb'dy in the near and far vicinity
Even the Oneness that is part of the Holy Trinity

Mercy what a mess that's creating
Just from running lips that's berating
Everyb'dy in the near and far path
Best get ready for an intolerable aftermath

This child stirs mess from beginning to end
Whether with a foe or a long time friend
Though everyb'dy in the near and far distant
Keeps moving to forbade any coexistence

I hope someb'dy hears my warning signs
All I hear is the voice sounding like mine
What happened to the ones near and far away
Was it something that they heard me say

About subjects that deal with daily mess
Whether it's someone's least or the best
I hope that child will soon be set straight
So I can close this wide big messy gate

Hambone on Sunday

Got my Sunday go to meetin' clothes on
And I'm just 'bout ready to go
With my keys in my hand
Then I looked at that ole Hambone
And stop dead in my tracks
But quickly turned and didn't look back
Got to the church and sat with the saints
Heard the preacher say have mercy — mercy on us
I tried hard to hear and follow the Word with trust
But my mind kept racing with real Sunday disgust
Like water flowing out a bucket full of holes from rust
So I said to myself I best pray for forgiveness
Speculating on how to stop this day of mess
So I joined the saints' moan and did my very best
The same image kept coming into view without rest
The preacher said kneel — kneel on your Sunday knee
And pray — pray hard for what's needed to set sin free
I followed the preacher's command best as can be
Still I'm wond'ring about that ole Hamboneshank
While everybody was praising and giving thanks
Depositing Sunday prayers into no earthling banks
All I could think about was that ole Hamboneshank
Then a saint confessed that nothing was too big or small
For the one on Sunday we call our everyday all and all
I sprang to my feet and shouted and hollered
That Hamboneshank didn't want my turnips but collards
A vision appeared as clear as the day was a church Sunday
Hamboneshank wouldn't be around to hassle my Monday
For there is a blessing in the words of a saintly prayer
Even when something like a Hambone creates despair
Others might wonder is this situation about greens
Or is ole Hambone in wait of another Sunday queen

Red Riding Hood

Listen before you go
Instructions to saying no
Listen to the voices
Before making choices

Hear what I say
Traveling on your way
Beyond hearing one can pray
While knitting a mindset to stay

An angelic form wickedly pleas for your soul
Distorting limits to gain your total control
Look into the eyes to see how they glare
In spite of the manifestation of despair

Filter the sounds that vibrate the air
Pocketing the familiar tones of care
Notice the cloaked helpful hand
Its mastermind is the wolf's plan

Yield to the pathway set before you
Not just the ones scented brand new
Keep the range of decipherable tones
When about you dry marrow in the bones

Hearing the voices that instruct no
Connect wellbeing as an even flow
Analyze the sounds you hear as you go
Obedience gives joy to eternally know

September's Colors

Red
>   White
>>   &
>>>   Blue

Veneration for those who died without a fight
Reminding everyone of humanity's waste
Due to an act of hatred made in unguarded haste

We wear the colors of national unity
For people in a sad world community
Death for an unknown reason
Pains **US** from season to season

Red
>   White
>>   &
>>>   Blue

Forever present in our daily sight
Surpassed by pain vividly shown
On the love ones' faces left alone

We will always wear the colors

Red
>   White
>>   &
>>>   Blue

A reminder of peace we must pursue

A Cup of Coffee

A cup of coffee is a nickel
I paid and wished for more
Down in my belly it tickles
Jumpstarting from ceiling to floor

Returning thoughts of similar pay
The price changed to a dime
Bought it 'cause its coffee day
No matter if it differs from other times

Seemingly the price changed again
A cup of coffee is now a quarter
Bought it and used the sipping plan
Savoring the content in pouring order

Puzzled yet at another change
A cup of coffee cost fifty cents
And the flavor isn't rearranged
Paid as if I owned money-mints

By now there's a cry for help
A cup of coffee cost a dollar
I drank it as I slowly wept
Change again and I'm gonna holler

From a nickel
To a dime
From a dime
To a quarter
From a quarter
To fifty cents
From fifty cents

Evelyn Dilworth-Williams

To a dollar

A cup of coffee is a dollar plus
Yet I sip while I make a fuss

So here's to you ENRON, WORLDCOM
All you CEO's and other exec's
The question is: *What price is next?*
A query to those of brewing suspect

Songs from the Morning: what will this day bring

I Sing

My gratitude is in the song I sing
All that you give pleasure it brings

Lord I sing my song to Thee
Lord I sing, Lord I sing

The melody is heard with the heart
Lord, this song will never depart

Lord I sing my song to Thee
Lord I sing, Lord I sing

My faith in Thee is in the song that I sing
For your precious blood is everlasting

Lord I sing my song to Thee
Lord I sing, Lord I sing

Comfort comes when I sing praises to Thee
Knowing you are there set my spirit free

Lord I sing my song to Thee
Lord I sing, Lord I sing

Sunday Moaning

Yeah! Lord, I hear your plea
This ole world was made for me

'Cause you wanted company to see
Though I opt to be set free

Still I'm goin' make it through your gates
'Cause I've been a steppin' so as not to be late

Yeah! Yeah! Yeah! Lord

I believe in all that you say
Just trying to ask if I still may

Be the servant that will obey
So as to be with you on judgment day

Yeah Lord! Yeah! Yeah!

Converted

I've been with my Savior and I feel brand new
When I'm with Him the old I'll no longer pursue

My hands are extended to all of man
For my heart has made a fresh start
My eyes plainly see what others mean to me

I've been with my Savior and I feel brand new
When I'm with Him the old I'll no longer pursue

My feet travel the right way
My mouth knows exactly what to say
The Word my ears clearly hear
And I receive it without worldly fear

I've been with my Savior and I feel brand new
When I'm with Him the old I'll no longer pursue

Evelyn Dilworth-Williams

MIDDAY

Life expectations with the reality of hope
that safeguards our morning promises

Myth or Truth?

Squandering beneath the blaze of the sun
Magnifies the unlimited from the great beyond
While all that's to do is to share our humanity
Balancing fidgeted desperation of life's insanity

Purloiner

I am the seed that was stolen away
Though hundreds of years made this day
I'm trying to forgive as I bow to pray
My soul seeks my missing life to portray

Unfulfilled chambers of my heart
Retracts from the beats of my forced start
My many mothers' voices steadily impart
The fertile grounds of my life's seed-depart

I wonder what it feels like to be at home
Nestle in the truest spirit of ancestral bones
And not having to search for a place to roam
My essence of life would ne'er share being alone

Here in a land where my history must stay
Replacing the realness of my life's yesterday
That is now distant as the Milky Way
'Cause I am the seed that was stolen away

My America Too!

America affords the venue for a life that's good
With fear and idleness in actual fact not understood
Taking simple resources and make into delicacies
Self-framing them as unique upgrades past tendencies

When a former slave starts a school as a college
To equalize the use of once forbidden knowledge
That will sustain through the course of passing time
Only in America can one make such a radical climb

America's doors to prosperity swing both ways
Evidence is there when we review the life of slaves
From the dinner table with servings of hog intestines
To this day are accepted as a delight that was predestined

We can go to foreign lands and fight side by side
Return home and the relationships immediately subside
Only in America will you return to the battlefields
Abandoning home grown rancor to be later revealed

Evelyn Dilworth-Williams

America is an inimitable home-based whether straight or bent
Her design is an indigenous, self-determined, shackled content
With such a variety she spun into a land with freedom to dissent
Not by her doings but with the divine power that's heavenly sent

Where in the world is there another America
So protected by all those of valiant might
Keeping her charge forever in plain sight
Giving the world freedom's timeless light

What a land!!!
           A land
                That will forever stand
                          A claim of pride to
live as an American

The Chariot

I hear the songs my people use to sing
Lyrics that tell me freedom has a sting
Denied to some and to others it clings
I hear the songs my people use to sing
Their voices come with earth's silence
Yet I sing the songs with my resonance
I sing the songs my people use to sing
Their voices are hushed
But I sing and ne'er rushed
Swing Down; Swing Down Sweet Chariot
And Let Me Ride
I can hear'em singing
About the *Chariot* coming to the low side
'Cause their humanness was coldly denied
Where the cott'n was planted and picked
And where my people lived and died
The *Chariot* needed to swing low
Taking 'em to a worthy life to bestow
Swing Down Sweet Chariot; Sweet Chariot
Swing Down
Where the cott'n blossoms beckoned for their hand
And the lash marks on their bodies were greed of man
The songs kept strength from leaving their backs
No matter how long they carried cott'n picking sacks
I sing the songs 'cause I too am signaling the *Chariot*
Not from the low land of the cott'n field
But the neighborhood ghetto where I live
From the low rent district on my side of town
Where there're chalk outlines on the cement ground
That takes account of my people's personal hand
To the akin sisters and brothers of the Motherland
Who sing songs without the ancestral plan

Still I sing the songs my people use to sing
Honoring voices that are hushed
Today I sing— I sing and ne'er rushed

Swing Down Sweet Chariot; Swing Down
Swing Down
By the cellblocks on the low side to get the young
'Cause they too are singing that same ole song
So many of them are in need of a *Chariot* ride
A ride to a place so freedom won't be denied
Swing Low Sweet Chariot and Let Us All Ride
For that's where you'll find us on the low side
Swing Down Sweet Chariot; Swing Low
That's the song we as a people still know
The starters' voices are hushed
The song is sang and ne'er rushed
Equal opportunity is the beauty of the ride
A reason for singing from the low side
Knowing I too can get a *Chariot* ride
Swing Down Sweet Chariot; Swing Down
Better as I stand ready with self-earned pride
Meeting those whose freedom was ne'er alive
I can hear 'em singing to give that child a ride
Sweet Chariot Swing Low; Sweet Chariot Swing Low
For I've got a ways to go; for I've got ways to go
Swing Low, Swing Low, Swing to the Low Side

Jana Braids Ceerea's Hair

Plaited hair and natural curls
Made identity plain to see
Crowning the top of the girls
Knowing who each would be

Just a thought of the mind
With an order for the day
Springing forth a clear kind
Replacing tedious play

Plaited hair swinging in the wind
Appearing to await the daily call
Running to meet an all timed friend
From a voice that thought of it all

The wind blows through her curls
As the call is the only sound heard
Coming from just one of the girls
The other is in a state that's blurred

Constructing the life that awaits
The future is a few days ahead
Knowing time passed to hesitate
Diminishing play to void instead

The creation of selected advice
With voices that speak to her soul
A life only for those in her sight
And no other binding her control

Planning for the day of separation
Paths leading to make living choices

Confirming life's timed dedication
While listening for the created voices

One speaks with braids resting placid
The other with curls made with care
Unwinding life's fear as time masks it
Replacing it with wisdom's timed-share

There's a sound from a familiar tone
Sufficient stay of a day's mind ingestion
Tomorrow comes with sameness shown
Holding wrangling voices of suggestions

The Grand Dame

Pardon me please
How do you do *madam*
Sho do like *yo* looks today
Wouldn't mind an invite to stay

Pardon me please
I mean no harm
Don't fret or get alarm
Just want to meet a friend
That will let me come in

Pardon me please
Oh don't get upset
I know we just met
A vision like you
Is what I must pursue

Pardon me please
I know I'm persistent
Sho am sorry about your resistance
It is jest you I want to get to know
'Cause you're such a splendid show

Pardon me please
Why do you never respond to me
I've been pleading as much as can be
Still you never turn in my direction
This is a painful ego spirit rejection

Evelyn Dilworth-Williams

Pardon me please
I guess I'll just *git* along
I feel like I'm colossally wrong
Thinking like the huddled masses
That my presence integrates the classes

Pardon Me Please!!

Honey and Gall

Outward passivity
Quells the flame
That burns the body
While the heart bleeds the same

The show of pearly whites
Give surety to life maintained
With fewer endured lashes
Swaying tomorrow's pain

Too Passionately Intense

Rockets glaring
Bombs bursting
Flags flying
Marchers marching
Mantra of songs
A time to remember
In infamy
Ne'er to not remember
The price was too high
The nation's birth
A celebration of
Life's Passion,
Liberty and
Pursuit of Happiness
A time to embrace
An unyielding pledge
To protect— honor with
Loyalty and pride
It happened
It's remembered
An award-winning
Moment in time
For freedom's sake
Ne'er to not remember
The huddle masses
In the belly of the
Slave carriers
That sameness of intensity
The mind is aflame
Relentless hold
With jaws of a whale
And the grip of a lion

Ne'er to not remember
The price was too high
Too many lives
Too many deaths
Sacrifice too high
For too many years
It happened

It's remembered
For freedom's sake
Times that ne'er fade
The price was too high
Be it
Independence celebration
Or pilgrimages
To the motherland
We can ne'er not remember
The price was too high
The mind and heart
Store and protect
The manageability
To factor reoccurrence
To the denomination
Of naught
We must all
Remember
To ne'er forget!

The Melting Pot

The acceptability of a papyrus melting pot
Embraces the theme for a worthy plot
Written exactness is without doubt
Read and spread throughout

Etched in the foundation of a nation
And acknowledged throughout generations
While the vociferous candor of its formulators
Includes a hollow introduction about the Creator

Praiseworthy is the content of the ideology
Culpable is the reality of its chronology
Confound by such unknown solemnity
The pot is torched by the lack of civilized gravity

The melting pot includes all of man's kind
With the exception of a heart of the mind
All that we melt will forever flame and burn
Unless the heart melts for us to share and learn

Melting into one is so easy to write and record
To apply the Master's Word keeps it from void
For sharing a thought of each others' lives is a major feat
Still blending of hearts causes man's humanity to n'er retreat.

For the heart harnesses the love
And can melt one into an angelic dove
The true melting pot of life can exist in our earthly space
By stirring the Master into the melting pot of the human race

Needing the Past

History must be preserved:
Not out of fury
Not out of odium
Not out of pity
Not out of remorse
Not out of spoils
Not out of wrath
Not out of trends
Not out of vengeance
Not out of fear
Not out esteem
and
Not out of order
for
Fury promotes inner rage
Limiting the spirit of peace
Odium destroys reconciliation
Stifling the spread of love
Pity denies self-growth
Retarding self motivation
Remorse fertilizes guilt
Defense becomes forefront
Spoils are never shared
Continuation of obstruction
Wrath limits reconstruction
Wasted productive time
Trends last for a short while
Obscuring permanent harmony
Vengeance overwhelms reason
Repeating the same mishap
Fear allows the same control
Disavowing decision-making

Evelyn Dilworth-Williams

Esteem disfigures reality
Treating others like inferiors

Whatever one's history might be
From a rebel flag flying
To singing, "My Country Tis of Thee"
Our ancestors paid by dying

Awarding the future a history
The past comes with a price
Leaving life beyond a mystery
Aborting moral mayhem twice

The Spirit of Africa

Africa's spirit is rooted in my soul
Never to abscond my sense of being
Though no similitude of times long ago
Before self identity's birth exit fleeing

The spirit of Africa never leaves my soul
Africa's presence drenches my senses
Seemingly far beyond my rational control
Leaving my thoughts with Africa's defenses

Negro

Wide eyes
     Shaking knees
          Disfigured frame
From head to toe
Visibility
Of a person
Becoming a Negro
Cargo transported from the Mother Land
With buried treasure
Oblivious of its measure
A mixture of sameness of a similar clan
Creating through the course of human time
That which will generate treasures to unveil
A fusion's return of acknowledged prime
From the distant shores of the first to set sail
For there it was in obscure view
The appearance of that captured soul
Hid the possessions of the future to hold
Not even the carriers of the seeds knew
Still its cargo made its journeyed way
Evading daily the moment of death's second
Making an appearance of a coming day
Just lying in wait redeeming time to reckon
Though forcefully rendering to an anew
Hoarding living treasures for life to pursue
Though masked out of human view
Still secretly in wait for time's rescue
Bending and bowing to gallantly protect
That which anyone took time to detect
An emerging treasure that others neglected
Sons and daughters through time revealed
Humanity's spirit splendid strength of will

Feelings from '63

The clothes got wet but not the souls
From the forceful pouring of the hoses
The spirits were ne'er dampened
Though evil attempts were rampant
Flames were fueled and denied shame
To lay hands on the real aged old blame

Overcoming second class citizenry
Ne'er use the killing children bombs

We march
      We sing
            We cry
No more
      No more
            No more

'Cause we're ready to die
Believe it and that's no lie
Change the guard
Here comes a new age start!

Evelyn Dilworth-Williams

The Water Hose of 1963

Pressure from the moments of time
Spewed an intolerable gush of pain
Drenching a humankind-inferno
With a straight fire hose weapon
That no longer adhered to intent

Designed to abate the combustion
Of pain sorrow and hope
The projectile of the hose
Aimed its purpose on those
Lives that couldn't be consoled

The high pressure of the moment
Warranted a high pressure weapon
That didn't blast like dynamite
Yet used to abort the peaceful fight
For freedom's wrongs into right

The water hose's deterministic chaos
Set aflame a stir within the human spirit
That refused to smolder or extinguish
The non-combatants to relinquish
An unfamiliar mindset so distinguish

The sound of rushing water
Ejecting from a high powered hose
Ne'er deterred the committed stance
No matter what the moment's glance
At the painful momentarily circumstance

The water hose had its might
But no match for what was in sight

Freedom from mankind's disgrace
For an entire socially deprived race
That was claiming its rightful place

Oh the hose discharged with vengeance
Ripping clothing and flesh all at once
Still the inner spirit wouldn't concede
The hose- recipients stayed on their knees
'Til living water poured from eyes of people freed

The 63's

The day with the unsuspected purpose
With the sun in its rightful position
Gleaming with an awareness of my existence
Showing face of my prior conception's assignment
Yet a day masked as an ordinary pathway
And all familiarity was at its baseline
Perennials scents and visions propagated
Awaiting the truth of the moment in time
Where would I go what would I do
The mindset controls were far beyond me
For within my reach came into being
The day I faced my destiny from inside life's soul
Shaping one day as if it were the original's last
The centenarian perils bursting my heart filled heart
While the ripen moment disjointed from its crippled start
The birth of *1863* fractured impropriety of an unwanted past
Still something was more essential than nothing
A malnourished existence with need of more
With hands demanding a balance of the day
An unpretentious proactive mission evolved naturally
The task to fill the ordained orders came about
With more than man's vision controlling the way
1963 took its course in the history of humankind
Yoking the centenarian perils with no fear or resolutions
The walk for a balance summoned the courageous
Whether it was a self or heavenly designed
The season for familiar scents and visions
Grabbed hold with an untamed newness of survival
The bare essentials of life's daily run
Changed the order of a century's sun
The unawareness of the day changed its scent
And reality's timed vision was God's intent

What Is the Question?

Where are you black boys?
I don't see many of you on the streets
Are you hiding thinking you're beat
Where are you…?
I went to the colleges and universities and I saw a few
There're more, I saw your Mama crying as if she knew
I stopped by the house of prayer
And I didn't find many there
Where are you…?
I searched America's corporations
And found too few in that situation
Too afraid to compete
Thinking once again you'll get beat
Where are you…?
I visited the family homes
And the women folk were all alone
With no man head of their thrones
Looking overworked to the bones
Where are you…?
You seemed to have vanished
Into being street clannish
Your disappearance is outlandish
Seemingly you leaped and banished
Where are you…?
I went to the hospital rooms
And the numbers of you increased
Was told it was greater but many are deceased
And the ones left there are left with gloom
Where are you…?
I decided to tour the military
The numbers in each branch varied
Tallied the sum and didn't get much

Can't help to wonder what caused such
Where are you…?
I've searched high and low
I can't find where you'll show
'Cause every where I go I see just a few
There're more, I saw your Mama crying as if she knew

Where are you…?
Let me stop by the jail
Before I get too frail
From looking for that black boy
Whose Mama couldn't post his bail
Are— you— here…?

The New World

Huddling with the masses yearning to breathe free
With chains and locks from my head to my feet
Was the sanity that embodied all of me
Self-guarding my spirit was all that wouldn't retreat

The stench of human bondage weakens my innate shell
Creating a ghost from time that once freely roamed
To the demise of the person prior to the criminal sail
Ne'er to be the same inborn poor flesh and tired bones

New genetic spirits evolved with notoriety
Desecration from the sameness of others
With a mindset beyond visible sobriety
Residuals for the masses sailing as brothers

Effen

Effen I don't know where I've been
How do I know where I can go
And where my station in this universe *be*
Effen I don't know where I've been
How do I step over inequities breaking free

I've got to know my journey's course
And whether to bed that same force

I've got to know the hurdles I've jumped
Enabling me to stay course-trumped

I've got to know the road I trod
In the event there's a man-made chastening rod

I've got to know who was taken to the slaughter
Passing on its avoidance to my son and daughter

I've got to know my earthly stay
For the coming of the new generation's day

I've got to know where my ancestors' tears fell
No matter *effen* their remains are in heaven or hell

I've got to know *effen* happiness took hold
And grab it to keep my life story in my control

I've got to know my ancestors' past
To keep my survival mode steadfast

So, *effen* I don't know where I've been
How is it I know where I *be*

The story must be forever told
And must be forever heard
Halting inhumanity from aging old

Evelyn Dilworth-Williams

Mother Africa: We Shall Meet Again

Moans
      Groans
My children are gone
Never seen again
Who mastered this plan

A sense of distance
Captures my resistance
That my children are gone
My heart beats alone

Where did they go
Will I ever know
Cross that big sea
Far away from me

My children are gone
I feel it in my bones
Where on earth could they be
Now I'm searching heaven to see

State of Affairs

My fellow sisters and brothers
Today's yesterday is where I stand
With perplexities in my heart and hand
Wondering why I'll help my own demise
Perchance myself I've conditioned to despise
Knowing I'm last hired and first fired
Birthing the rooting-system of my blues
While a sister or brother with intent misuse
Affirmative Action
Here today gone tomorrow
Raising children to bring sorrow
When I move in others move out
Yet it's my kind that I fatally doubt
My neighborhood steadily deteriorates
Though taxed with collective mandates
The design of a colorless configuration
However I'll turn my back on my relations
Dope crosses the borders of this land
Synthesizing my neighborhood's gland
Less than nothing to stop the flow
Of the sale to the kin people I know
Jail cells house too many people of color
My input retreats just as the others
Lending institution rejects my applications
My money is used in their daily calculations
The neighborhood stores sell inferior stock
Still that is where I always hasten to flock
Systemically depreciated of my best intentions
While ditching a brother's supportive interventions
The sting is no longer an unrelated bearer
My image of my hue is the notorious carrier
Pitifully moaning as I self inflict daily pain

Evelyn Dilworth-Williams

As others denounce the innate merit of my brain
Birthing the help to hurt my sisters or brothers
As the task breeds in the palm of those and others
Why apply and work and master a job already filled
With sweaty-bloody tears that my people-kind spilled
The abandonment of life's potency of my ego ideal
A sad *State of Affairs* that "I" oxygenate to make real

Whose Sons?

Shame on us! Shame on us!
Whom will he trust?

Growing up like a impious weed
Early disbarment of his manhood
Lacking in provisions to succeed
His being never fully understood
Paying his maturation any mind
Expecting him to be the best kind

Shame on us! Shame on us!
Whom will he trust?

Left alone to figure out life too long
Expecting too much and giving too little
Crippling his soul to never grow strong
Making his life an unanswered riddle
Changing his innate spirit of peace
To growing anger as his days increase

Shame on us! Shame on us!
Whom will he trust?

Giving up when his lot in life declines
Rarely extending a hand of a loving stroke
Liability free for his choices of the mind
Unaware of the time that his spirit broke
Demanding that his frailties were his alone
Oblivious of love that's inadequately shown

Shame on us! Shame on us!
Whom will he trust?

Self- unacceptability besieges his existence
He attacks all that's identical when seeing
Diminishes the will of evil's resistance
Annihilates his reminded self being
His values in life are learned from us
Shame! Shame! Whom will our sons trust?

Amen! Amen!

Amen! Ize kin stand on m'feet
Amen! Ize got my own sum teet
Amen! Doz da lashes dun heel
Amen! Eben dough Ize wuz nilly kill
Amen! Ize gotz me a gument represent
Amen! Hez wuz a god-sent
Amen! Dat ole war iz all ober
Amen! De people seams lak daz sober
Amen! Ize freed nigh freed as a burd
Amen! My prayers wuz findly hurd
Amen! Amen! Amen!

Songs from the Midday: when morning fades into real life

Mightier Than Man

My soul rejoices that something is mightier than man
The might that I praise will forever stand

His precious might uses the wind as His wings
And can make something as tiny as a mockingbird sing

O' my soul rejoices that something is mightier than man

The clouds are His chariots that appear at His command
And His travels are spread all over this land

His forgiveness extends beyond everlasting
And the greatest of love he gives by just asking

O' my soul rejoices that something is mightier than man

The might I praise is forever heavenly grand
O' my soul rejoices that something is mightier than man

Don't Worry I'm Never Alone

When you see me walking
and I seem to be walking alone
Don't you worry –
'cause I'm walking with the One-
who sits on the high throne
That same One who carried the cross
on his back to Calvary alone
For He never, never leaves me alone
Never alone, thank you Master,
never alone

When you see me crying,
and I seem to be crying alone
Don't you worry-
'cause my tears are wiped-
by the one who sits on the high throne
That same One who wore a crown of thorns
on His head alone
For He never, never leaves mc alone
Never alone, thank you Master,
never alone

When you see me burden
and I seem to be burdened alone
Don't you worry –
'cause I'm with the burden bearer
the one who sits on the high throne
That same One who was pierced in the sides alone
For He never, never leaves me alone
Never alone, thank you Master,
never alone

When you see me broken
by the hands of time
and I seem to be broken alone
Don't you worry –
'cause my brokenness is mended
by the One who sits on the high throne
That same One who refused to save Himself,
and endured the pain alone
For He never, never leaves me alone
Never alone, thank you Master,
never alone

When you see me confused
and I seem to be confused alone
Don't you worry –
'cause my confusion is cleared
by the one who sits on the high throne
That same One who hung His head
and died for you and me alone
For He never, never leaves me alone
Never alone, thank you Master,
never alone

When you see me walking in darkness
And my way seems void and unsafe
Don't you worry –
'cause my darkness becomes the light
by the one who sits on the high throne
That same One who rose from the dead
and soared to His Father's arms alone
For He never, never leaves me alone
Never alone, thank you Master,
never alone

Evelyn Dilworth-Williams

The Shepherd

The Lord is the Shepherd of my soul
Granting me energy I need to hold
Earth's wisdom steering me to heaven's control
The Lord is the Shepherd of my soul
Guiding me through snares of danger untold
And stretching His hand for me to grab hold
For the Lord is the Shepherd of my soul

Sometimes when my course is all confused
Taking for granted how His Word should be used
He turns to guide me and never does He refuse
The Lord is the Shepherd of my soul
Whether a stormy day or a sunny one
He walks with me just like I'm His son
For the Lord is the Shepherd of my soul

When I start my beginnings without Him in sight
And pretend my walk is of my own delight
He prods my spirit to show me His loving might
The Lord is the Shepherd of my soul
Willing to let me stumble so I can grow
But never leaving me for the world's foes
For the Lord is the Shepherd of my soul

He is the Lord, the Shepherd of my soul
The Shepherd is the Lord
He is the Lord, the Shepherd of my soul
The Shepherd is the Lord

So Glad for My Cross

I'm so glad I had to struggle with my cross
For when it was over I no longer felt lost

My story is for all especially the downtrodden
For my Savior never lets me be forgotten
Don't be dismayed by life's treacherous journey
My Savior will comfort you throughout eternity

I'm so glad I had to struggle with my cross
For when it was over I no longer felt lost

My struggle strengthens my belief
And hands me my needed relief
Victory appears when I am at my weakest point
It is then the Savior uses His power to anoint

I'm so glad I had to struggle with my cross
For when it was over I no longer felt lost

Don't feel like a misfit or a helpless stranger
All who come His way have to cross over life's danger
The struggle makes your weary soul tired to the bone
But keep believing and your reward awaits you at His throne

I'm so glad I had to struggle with my cross
For when it was over I no longer felt lost

Evelyn Dilworth-Williams

Sharing the blessing of His merciful power
Gives me time to confess each day every hour
Peace is granted to me after I give up control
It's the blessing I can't keep it must be told

I'm so glad I had to struggle with my cross
For when it was over I no longer felt lost

E
V
E
N
I
N
G

Mounting or waning chances of points of thanks; with matching or un-matching of a day's desires

Evelyn Dilworth-Williams

My Evening Song:

Whether I'm there or not!

Rose early this morning with a full day ahead
Had all sorts of thoughts running through my head
Stopped to give praise for allowing me to get out of bed
& filled with the spirit to tackle life's daily dreads

Interacting with my love ones and feeling so wondrously blessed
Could hardly restrain myself from shoutin' while getting dressed
Knowing this time was an accurate measurement with no space for
jest
I just praised Him for giving me a new day after a good night's rest

The day moved in its direction without any effort on my part
Looked around and half of what was there was preparing for
tomorrow's start
Rushing to make do with what was left of the time as if it would
never restart
Overwrought my mind and stifled good choices that I still needed
to impart

Running frantically on half empty and with lots of things left to do
Made me mindful of the tomorrows and that each day was brand new
Settling my mind that part of today will give tomorrow something to pursue
And that the preparation for each day will always relentlessly continue

Whether I'm there or not!

So I'll just sing my songs of praise…

Never in doubt of His power, not even amazed.

Change

When the mind sheds harnessed feelings of cold
Newness grabs the spirit for another seasonal hold
Moisten air perfumed the untamed scent of spring
Beneath the cumulus a flock of robins melodiously sing

Bursting with an array of brilliant flowers
Life's time demands understood showers
Dawning on this burst of spanking energy
An outlay of change becomes our synergy

Evelyn Dilworth-Williams

Flight

Never a dull moment
When in the presence
Of birds with wings
Whether it be a
Red, Brown, Blue
White, Green, Purple
Black or
Yellow...
Joy, Peace & Love the birds' journey brings
Ceasing when breathing life without wings

stainless wonder

when tears are shed
and fall to the ground
there's vivid proof that
no one is around

no arms, no shoulders, no hands
to soothe the pain
so tears fall
never to make a stain

no ones' there to share despair
the tears roll and settle down
onto the maker of the ground
no touches from strokes to share

Evelyn Dilworth-Williams

The Ground

No shoulder to lean on
No arms that embrace
No hands to wipe the tears away
Standing in pain with life's dismay
Tears fall to the ground
'Cause no one is around
Can't share tears of despair
Can't make a stain
So they just fall to the ground
'Cause no one is around
No touch
No embrace
No strokes
Just dismay
From tears of the day
With vivid proof of no one around
An unshed tear
Without anyone near

The Sea's Tides

The tides emerge without doubt
Rushing or waning in appearance
From the Sea of Life assigned setting
With perception to earth's indigenous

They come with fair or unfair warning
Regardless of who is or is not prepared
The tides must obey the command
From a disconnected starting place

Willingly accepting the tide's reality
Makes the day a life of experiences
With sometimes or not understanding
The gravity of a day's forthcoming truth

Preparation to withstand the phenomenal
Procures investments of the soul's attention
Lessening the light of interested matters
Re-shifting to the intensity of the Sea of Life

The steps are manifested accordingly sensed
With the assignment of godly-made status
An assignment of the daily tide's strength
Fortifying the realism of personal values

Creating tides that construct self worth
With hands that gird beyond or within
Reaching from the inner person's space
Humbling tides to ownership control
The Sea of Life eternally flows
Harnessing concentrated destinations
Strengthening less to a final birth of a day
Rushing or waning to self allotted space

The Whistler

The sound of the whistling wind
Highs and lows come from all directions
Conceding wonderment from beginning to end
With senses seeking its pulsating connections

The note of sounds requires attention
Breezing rhythmically beyond measure
By the wind maker earthly intentions
With its unique hidden vocal treasure

The sounds display a complex task
Only to guess its start to end
As the whistler maintains its mask
Creating astonishment within

Never to see the true embodiment
Nor the casting of a real silhouette
Still I know it is living sound intent
Coming and going without any regret

Evelyn Dilworth-Williams

Troubling Times

The setting of the sun
Leaves a promise undone
Mending peace for no one
Except God's only Son

The seedbed of life
Is the earth's strife
Negotiating for peace
Must in no way cease

Miracles

The sunbeam calibrations
Striking the earth's surface
Exactness in its calculations
Nourishing life's daily pace

Starry nights after a storm
Sparkling beyond human sight
Dials without hands or alarms
Extricating that is of fright

Hearts robotically mending
Prior breakage of tiny pieces
Adhesive bond of sending
No manpower releases

Life's wounds somehow heal
With an invisible command
That's at will timely revealed
The strokes of heaven's hand

Clouds bursting in a day
Moistening with effortless ease
Life's dryness goes away
Rendering a life to please

The wholeness of man
Amazement shows face
Repeats itself time again
With a life of accepted grace

Evelyn Dilworth-Williams

The Speaker

Stood at the podium
A thunderous clap of hands
Took a bow
And the speech began

New presenter
Old words
All that was spoken
Was previously heard

Different voice
Similar sentences
New theory
Aged variables

New resources/technology:
From index cards
Pointer and screen
Slide projector
With/without a carousel
An overhead projector
With transparencies
And a special writing pen
From the copier/computer
A print out for everyone
Power point
With music
And....

Yet:
Presenter presents in a different way
Still we breathe the same each day

For all that we hear others say
Hopefully makes the earth a better stay

Evelyn Dilworth-Williams

Cora Belle's Missing Friend

A flowery dress with brand new matching shoes
Can't look away from herself; her eyes are glued

Chewing gum and laughing loud
Beckoning for the worldly crowd

Making friends with all kinds
Searching hard to rob 'em blind

Her actions never make her shame
The greater the vices the greater the fame

Until she meets the master of the game
Leaving her chewing gum and looking lame

'Cause that friend of Cora Belle
Is now sitting in the county jail

Cora Belle was prayerfully blessed
Wise enough not to pay mind to mess

She turned her life around
Noticing a friend go down

Still Cora Belle dresses to kill
Wearing fine things that she doesn't steal

Walking and looking at herself while chewing
Embracing friends that are worth pursuing

Cora Belle's lessons in life were hard learned
Spending time with those that got her burned

'Cause friendship lessons don't come trouble-free
Cora Belle is my friend that would readily agree

Evelyn Dilworth-Williams

Enough

Collard greens
Venison stew
Butter beans
& Cornbread too

Meal for a king
Red grape wine
Best of everything
As I sip and dine

Eating and drinking
Un-clouding my mind
Getting full and thinking
Lest my work gets behind

Eating all I can get
Food diminishes after sunset
My body will slumber to rest
Re-starting tomorrow at my best

With enough leftovers:
Collard greens
Venison stew
Butter beans
& Cornbread too

Flight of Joy

Never a dull moment
In the presence of birds
With wind filled wings
Whether: red, blue, black,
White, green, purple, orange,
Or speckled
Joy the birds bring
Only to cease
When breathing
With folded wings

The Chosen Samaritan

Boldly I stand against wrongful deeds
Embracing the cry of those with needs
A compassionate vessel through and through
Rendering service to upgrade life to anew

Replacing drawbacks with realities of what's good
Enhancing life for others as well as understood
Then nourishing inflicted wounds that scar a life
Obtaining betterment for those tormented with strife

Seemingly tired yet never do I get weary
For the misuse of others stirs an inner fury
That directs my strength to give help to others
A contented outcome for my sisters and brothers

The *"Good Samaritan"* is my life's example
Giving to the helpless that which is ample
For service is my gift embedded in my creed
So I hand it willingly and never concede

Kindred Keeper

My spirituality strengthens my waxed bones
Surrounded by life's feebleness I'm never alone
Fidelity in the supreme fortifies my expectations
While I'm exalting the reliance of God's creation

Faith is the keeper of my situation
So blessed to take care of my relations
Never spiritually improvised by my task
Always liberal responses are there when I ask

Confident that all will go well
Honored by the spirit's everlasting spell
Moreover basking in hope to give me peace
Knowing one day we'll all have relief

The spirit manifests daily assuring me success
Rejoice not in complaining lets me know I'm blessed
Rooted love assigned circumstances girds up my strength
Makes the pressure of the day short in time's length

Caring with faith, hope and charity comes from above
Yet all could be forgotten but never caring with love

Evelyn Dilworth-Williams

A Dry Tear

Clarity is before me
There is little pain
Outcomes I can see
In this sober frame

Vivid projections
The tears of sorrow
With heaven connections
Found no tomorrows

My eyes are clear
With the Savior drawn near
No crying down here
Just a dry tear

Today rules with clear eyes
From heaven's revision
That yesterday denied
Leaving endless vision

Sorrow

Sorrow is part of the emergence of a day
Bursting forth to assure a time to pray
Without regard for what others might say
Sorrow is the Master's attention getting way

Evelyn Dilworth-Williams

My Bag

Just an ole bag
That some call a hag
But don't be fooled
I'm really just cool

An ole bag
Sometimes called a hag
I'm cool
And ain't no fool

Now, a bag can be a hag
And my bag ain't no brag
'Cause I got plenty to say
'Bout what makes my day

Now, what's in my bag
Betcha won't find a hag
Let me take a little look see
To share with others 'bout me

I'll go to the bottom to see what I can find
Got to push pass lots of stuff that's all mine
'Cause you know I'm one of a kind
Specially made from heaven's design

Oh! Just look what I almost forgot
My first family with all the family's lot
Oh! How special a family can be
Stick by you long before you plea

My bag is not new and it can hold lots of stuff
So I can be ready when life gets a little rough

Let me see what's inside
Next is something that can't be denied
It's my bag within a bag
Covered with an ole timey rag

Oh! It's got some top secret stuff
Now you notice it's just big enough
'Cause life's been good to me
Since I put my trust in Thee

I got some church in here
Got sum love that's dear
Got a song to keep life from growing dim
That starts off with praises just for Him
Got lots of living reasons to say thanks
About things ne'er part of earth's banks

Now, I'm going to put that aside
And dig deeper to see what I sometimes hide
Well, well just look at this
It's something I need to resist

Toxic waste
Made in haste
That I need to alleviate
So I can concentrate
On the beauty of life's intake

Stumbling blocks and no peace
Holding grudges and no love
Pointing the finger and no kindness
Blaming others and no longsuffering

These things are weighting my bag down
I'm not going to carry these burdens around

They make this ole bag too heavy
Denying a goodness of grace's levy

Out! Out! Damned Spots
Now my load seems light and unfilled
I need something that's surreal
Made just for me
That's special as can be

Maybe a big black man
No, got one of those on hand
Children to raise
Too out of it for those days
Possibly another career
But the world would shiver in fear

Let me take another look
This bag still got my back in a crook
Oh! My, I forgot to take out worry
That's why people like me don't do life in a hurry

Now, the bag fits well as my style
Just enough in it to carry for awhile
I've got what I need to happily thrive
What's in my bag keeps me sanely alive

Now:
Don't you be fooled, I ain't nobody's hag
My strut is a real smooth zig zag
In and out and up and down without a drag
I *be* cool strutting with my designer's bag

My Songs from the Evening Day

Evelyn Dilworth-Williams

A Blessing for My Lord

I'm going to be a blessing for my Lord
I'll abide in the Word that's never void
Never void, the Word of my Lord
Praying for strength, that's needed for my daily task
Allowing the surrender of this ole human made mask

I'm going to be a blessing for my Lord
I'll abide in the Word that's never void
Never void, the Word of my Lord
I'll go to humanity's table without worldly made strife
Swallowing portions that mercifully cleanse my sin-filled life

I'm going to be a blessing for my Lord
I'll abide in the Word that's never void
Never void, the Word of my Lord
With love I'll forgive, forgive all my earthly brothers
Even the ones who sin, sin against me and each other

I'm going to be a blessing for my Lord
I'll abide in the Word that's never void
Never void, the Word of my Lord
I'll praise His name, His wonderful name for all to hear
And show my faith in Him with reverence of absent fear

I'm going to be a blessing for my Lord
I'll abide in the Word that's never void
Never void, the Word of my Lord
The Word is my guide, His everlasting Word is my guide
It lets me forever cling to His pierced blood stained side

Evelyn Dilworth-Williams

I'm going to be a blessing for my Lord
I'll abide in the Word that's never void
Never void, the Word of my Lord

Repentance

Lord I'm getting ready to pay my debt
I've been spendin' every since we met
It's you Lord the holder of my bill
Help me Jesus to prepare for your will

Looking at the mighty store of things
Believing in you causes me to cling
It's you Lord the holder of my bill
Help me Jesus to prepare for you will

Praising you makes so many things clear
Living your convictions draws You near
It's you Lord the holder of my bill
Help me Jesus to prepare for your will

The snares of life come and go
Your grace and protection always show
It's you Lord the holder of my bill
Help me Jesus to prepare for your will

Lord you are the keeper of my fare
Charging only what I didn't share
It's you Lord the holder of my bill
Help me Jesus to prepare for your will

Lord I'm getting ready to pay my debt
I've been spendin' every since we met
Clear my debt O'Lord I pray
It's your will as to what I'll pay

NIGHT

The gains and loses of the day with reflections of praises and sorrows

Keeping in Mind

That which imprints the soul's mind
Can be trace to the effects on humankind
Whether days short in length
Or days beyond bodily strength
Those recalled are few in life's count
For our stay has an assigned amount
The being of each passing day ne'er fades
Most are just pale to life's present shades
Still the residue of some energy is the same
And emerges as potent within life's frame
Charting the course throughout birth's journey
Settles the soul's pursuit for all eternity
That which is done to manage earth's quest
Are the choices that arise from the worst and best
For those portions eternally stain earth's stay
Becoming motionless time and remains that way
To always mark the remembrance of life
The soul is rewarded with imprints that entice

So many days... none can be tucked away

Life's Leaves

Nurtured by Mother Earth
A matchless life from birth
From a familiar type of tree
Giving leaves for all to see
Variety is absolutely unique

Nature creates an endless design
Leaves from one created tree kind
A splendid diversified foundation
Sameness in portioned deliberation
Nourishing the Archetype's creation

Together

My life needs more than mercy
I need His loving grace too
His matchless mercy and grace
Supply my soul with mercy
And comforts my spirit with grace
Sustaining my life's daily walk
Mercy coils from heaven above
Grace spirals from His abundant love
My life needs twice over protection
To attain heaven's one way direction
He extends His hand of mercy
Grabbing hold with His hand of grace
Making painstaking steps likely
Mercy comes from heaven above
Grace comes from His abundant love
Only mercy along with grace
Sustains my life's earthly pace
When one is not enough
He simplifies what is rough
Intertwining mercy and grace
Creating life's unchanged solace

Sufficient Revival

I heard footsteps coming toward me
An image appeared for me to see
I was embraced with such strong arms
Strange as it was I felt no harm

Movement from me was out of my control
For a revival of my being took a strong hold
The footsteps I continued to hear
For an appeared image is always near

While the mighty grasp of an embrace
Identified itself as the Master's grace
Now I walk in the same footsteps that came toward me
For I must go where the image wants me to be

Strongly gripped with shelter from fear
'Cause all is well for the Savior is here
My movement is abound with an eye sighted difference
For my soul has an apparent promised deliverance

Yet I hear footsteps from all directions
Only to follow those of grace's image of protection

Important Stay

Marking territory challenges the best of a day
Making known the existence of magnitude
Layering seeds to look back to see
The totality of what breathing requires
More than a mere rise each day
The existence of a daily walk
Never suffice the energy it creates
The need for an object of humanity
Requires an extension to portray
Time wanes original presence
Though the mark of existence never forbade
For the duplication of essence
Rises to make presence obey

Evelyn Dilworth-Williams

Time Snapped

Yet, good as it seems
Just the same as ever
While snapping beans
With a face so clever

Then a sudden change
Grabbing hold of us all
Mixed-up strikes again
Snapping beans just stall

All about seems confused
Puzzlement stops the snap
A return of time unused
Stalling with a mystic gap

A day's pace is unleashed
As unknown times increase
A face that time once release
Diminishing snapping peace

Rinsed Off

Consumed by the dust of life
Layered with bitter strife
That rarely releases a glee
Mimicking ways to flee
Prepare to rinse life's residues away
With the Word when I kneel to pray

?

Why must I feel the fire before I believe it's hot
Must I get burned to learn

Why can't I believe that fat meat is greasy
When just believing would be so easy

Bought sense is the best sense; without a guess
Yet, so expensive to pay for my life's mess

The Moment

Pain and sorrow
Create tomorrow

Happiness and pleasure
Create today's measure

Today becomes tomorrow
And happiness replaces sorrow

Beyond the Words

Words came to me that are not of my thought
Beyond earth's vision rarely have I sought

Aunt Paralee came by to visit me today
Words came from her quintessence for me to say

When I thought the words couldn't get any better
I felt a celestial nudge from another of Papa's sisters, Aunt Etta

Papa stood on cosmos shore watching the verbal design unfold
Then predicted how the words would take a final hold

The thoughts of my message quickly come and go
Hastily do I capture what I want others to know

Never a thought that I really claim
A prearrangement of my words by those named

Time

Time is months, years, and days
It's the gift we get for our stay

Now precious moments lie in giving
Within the inner spirit of the living

All that's given is to be received
Only for those who truly believe

The gift of time is serenely rendered
Forth-coming from the heavenly sender

Evelyn Dilworth-Williams

Lighthouse and My Path

A lighthouse blaze appears without human will
Beaming on my path that's narrow and dim
Only the Master's plan makes the light real
Line directly from heaven above by Him

The light shows my way when my course is diminished
Illuminated vision of choice emerges without human will
My path widens to complete my predestine finish
Making life's walk steady and genteel

The light flickers all through the day
Letting me know it will never go away
As long as I honor Him and pray to obey
The lighthouse of my path will always stay

Grace

Pondering about tomorrow is too much of a task for man
Just believe the Creator's grace is sufficient for our plan
Self-preparation for life is a valueless feat
It is God's grace that banishes all defeat

Grasping and panting when things go not our way
Forgetting not His grace is there when we pray
Concerns of the flesh yield not a worthy place
The spirit of life's peace is the bounty of His grace

Striving to do what is honorable and good
Is the result of grace so well understood
So bless be the man who seeks the Creator's space
For we are glorified only by His amazing grace

Evelyn Dilworth-Williams

Time's Indirect Route

This time was without a plan
Stunting what we understand
Only love captivates its hold
The days slip by out of control

Duality creates life's new rules
Just hands not any useful tools
Rising day-darkness in clear view
All is there nothing of use is new

Central units construct multi-visions
Replicating uncharted split-decisions
Answering with abortive corrections
The days of cure are still projections

Love with hope replaces all reality
A life anew demanding its totality
The image of courage awaits its way
To needs of a love one's end of day

Un-song Singing

Sing a song of an unseasonable flowery bloom
Sing a song of a child being an adult too soon
Sing a song with an elevated first soprano's voice
Sing a song with an alto's analogous singing choice
Sing a song where daily pain ponderously reeks
Sing a song where the heart dares to speak
Sing a song of shear living brotherhood
Sing a song of sameness never understood

A flowery bloom
Appearing too soon
Watched with childish gloom
With a face covered with pain
For givers of love choose to abstain
Sing a song to restore life's refrain
Sing a song to restore life's course again
Versed with brotherhood as the flavor
From the sameness of the singing Savior

Sing a song…
Sing a song…
Sing a song…

The darkness of the day makes for songs of the night

Evelyn Dilworth-Williams

Thank You, Lord

Thank you Lord for
all that I didn't pray for
I'm so glad you change
the seasons at your will
and love for me you instilled
I'm so glad
your love made me worthy

Thank you Lord for
all that I didn't pray for
I'm so glad the sun can shine
on a rainy day
and your grace lights the way
I'm so glad
your love made me worthy

Thank you Lord for
all that I didn't pray for
I'm so glad
the wind whistles through the trees
and you soothe my brow
when there's a need
I'm so glad
your love made me worthy

Thank you Lord for
all I didn't pray for
I'm so glad you allow the sun
to warm my being
and grow flowers with blooms for seeing
I'm so glad
your love made me worthy

Thank you Lord for
all I didn't pray for
I'm so glad
you gave me the sense to believe
and supplied my needs
before I was even conceived
I'm so glad
your love made me worthy

Thank You, Lord

Blessed

Lord I'm so glad to know that I'm blessed
When surrounded by the followers of evil
You show me the way to clear away upheaval
I just look to the heavens and there you stand
With deep-rooted grace and a stretched out hand

Lord I'm so glad to know that I'm blessed
The storms of life's agony and discomfort
Appearing without a warning of any sort
You rearrange the pain of time to yield less
Before I plea you give my spirit needed rest

Lord I'm so glad to know that I'm blessed
To have family and friends always by my side
With love in their hearts, soul, and eyes
My blessings are clear and can't be denied
For you are always there to steer and guide

Lord I'm so glad to know that I'm blessed
When others around me are struggling with life's stay
I'm so glad I know to call them by name when I pray
With the certainty that you know what they need
To conquer their defeat and graciously succeed

Lord I'm so glad to know that I'm blessed
Rising each day with a view of the newness of the sun
Knowing this is not by man but it's what you've done
So my path can have the light that's needed to walk your way
Your sunset lets me know to thank you for another blessed day

Lord I'm so glad to know that I'm blessed

Lighthouse Beam

There's a lighthouse beam that never grows dim
Its source of energy comes from Him
The prophets had it when they shared the Word
Spreading it into the uttermost corners to be heard

There's a lighthouse beam that never grows dim
My mother and father used it on a daily base
To light the way for theirs to receive His grace
My old grandma and grandpa had it too
Each understood what the light could do

There's a lighthouse beam that never grows dim
The lighthouse keepers fade by the days
Yet the light keeps a high beam and always stays
The lighthouse of my life gets its source from you
Shining on my life's course to guide me through

There's a lighthouse beam that never grows dim
Its source of energy comes from Him
A glowing beacon from the Great I AM
That forever shines on His slaughtered lamb

The Lighthouse Keeper

Born with a lighthouse to keep from veering wrong
It affords me the reasons to manifest and be strong
The beacon shines for my life's treacherous journey
Guiding and steering my course throughout eternity

I have a lighthouse Keeper that shows the way
And I praise Him— praise Him day by day
No matter what course I take along life's way
The lighthouse Keeper shines on me everyday

The lighthouse of my life never fails
I can depend on it wherever I sail
My Keeper's light guided me from birth
With a high beam even when ascending from earth

I have a lighthouse Keeper that shows me the way
And I praise Him— praise Him day by day
No matter what course I take along life's way
The lighthouse Keeper shines on me everyday

MORNING

AGAIN

Renewal of un-touched living slated as the time to try all over again

Sunrise Dreams

Watching the sunrise
With wise opened eyes
It energizes the soul
To take life's control

Sunrise dreams come with ease
The task surrenders to life's vitality
Making dreams into tomorrow's reality
Akin to an agreeable morning breeze

The sunrise gleams on a virgin slate
To capture the new-fangled dreams
No matter how out of favor it seems
The sunrise dreams are never too late

Though past noon comes to be
Dreams of the sunrise are the jubilee
As the freshness for the pending day
Sparks thoughts from the soul to obey

Morning Comes

Morning nudges you and opens your eyes
Softly stroking and claiming those alive
With a gift of time wrapped in hand
Granting a day of life to you once again
Allowing the noonday to stare in your face
Straight from above with the glow of grace
With time in between to set things right
Hoping to attain it before the dark of night
Still time reveals the memory of the day
With a plea for another morning to obey

Motionless Future

The newness of a day
Appears when night's away
The sun peaks over the horizon in the sky
And life is made visible to the human eye
A day springs forth granting time for change
Clinging to the past makes the present remain
New pending time is the past and present again

Evelyn Dilworth-Williams

The Beauty of Life

The flesh is exultant
And the soul is in sync
The result is love
Praises from heaven above

To help those in need
And it's passed to help others
Nurturing those with less
Everyone is richly blessed

Caring for the ills of life
Aborts the intent of cruel ideas
Harmony surfaces to forever reign
Letting peace descend as our gain

Appreciating the unfamiliar traits
Never anointed as an alpha glow
Embracing multi-differences in sight
Thus causing an immeasurable light

All is here for us on earth
A universal phenomenal gift
Stroking with touches of reality
Awaiting the claim of actuality

Showering in the beauty of love
Supernaturally from heaven above
There in the heavens— the answer is love
Earth's beauty of life from cosmos above

The Factor

The sands of time
Pour over what's mine
Though I seldom kneel
Yet your spirit is revealed

The tattered life still rejoices
'Cause I constantly hear your voice
Knowing that all is well
And I'm a daily distant from hell

Life Is Sweet

Thoughts are rampant
Decisions are vacant
Life is sweet, a flower blooms
Confusion takes hold
Naked energy
Refusing to be clothed
While the mind decays
Rusting and growing old
Too much time in the past
And fear about right now
Seemingly abandoned dreams
Creep to regain prominence
Rejected for lack of need
Life is sweet, a flower blooms
Thoughts are stale
Visions are blurred
Such daily decisions
With inner/outer spirit control
Life is sweet, a flower blooms
A flower blooms

A Sinner's Prayer

Dear Lord here I am
Take my hand
Make me a better man
Inclusive of your plan
Forbade my sins
That I'm always in
Take your time
To become mine
Let my breath be of relief
Avoidance of Satan beneath

My Ship's Boat

Sailing on a clear day
My target seemed not far away
Just around the bend
Awaited my journey's end

Sailing with my ship intact
Without danger to react
Made my voyage one of ease
With my travels I was pleased

My know of how to sail
On a clear day without fail
For my ship was all maintained
My destination I'd surely gain

Still a bafflingly wind surged in midair
My ship stalled in unmatched despair
While my destiny awaited me there
A leaky boat appeared from nowhere

Seemingly sinking was my appointed fate
For a leaky boat was not a ship's re-make
My challenge to sail was given its test
What I learned on my ship without a guess

My leaky boat won't sail the way
That my ship did on a clear day
A new modus operandi was at first hand
Needed to fulfill my destination's plan

My spirit searched for an anchor to depend
As I steered my leaky boat towards my desired end

The wind tossed me up, down, and all around
Still I sailed with what balanced the wind's sound

The ship that sailed on a clear day
Taught me sailing was not learned that way
All my useful know-how on how to sail
That ole leaky boat; tender to my avail

Steering a boat thought to be a ship
Its destination is made with the right grip
Mindful of all of the vessel's control
Of the sailing passengers' body and soul

Evelyn Dilworth-Williams

The Potter's Helper

Warmly fixed in the fold of my arm
Staring at the potter's helper's face
With gazing virgin eyes full of charm
Bonding to a love threaded with grace

Oh what plans I have for your future
Looking into yearning and trusting eyes
Knowing not all that's needed to nurture
You are the gift that I'm so much oblige

My instructions are not clear
Your stare for hope ne'er ceases
I'll rely on the potter without fear
As the potter's technique releases

Conscious of an accepting stare
Molding an inseparable love pair
From eyes that beckon for my care
To godly promises to always be there

Betterment

How good and how pleasant it is to dwell in unity with peace
The causes are everlasting and create a bond never to cease
The design of all fore mention is built not of our own intention
But exist only from the commands on high from the throne
The inequities of that which surfaces each promised day
Harnessed from beginning to end when all bow to pray
Chosen you are from the womb of your mother
Never to be satisfactorily doubted by any other

Evelyn Dilworth-Williams

The Shepherd's Helper

An awesome mission for just a mortal man
Charged with the call from the Master's plan
Touched with wisdom of one who's truly grand
Affords him the space to accept his life's stand

The beauty of his message is not self-thought
Calvary is where his inspiration was bought
Standing before all in need of the Word
Praying the prayer that the Almighty wants heard

He shouts the scripture and ends it with a moan
The ole devil's spirit leaps and back to hell it's gone
Delivering the sermon with a stomp of his feet
Energizes him to battle evil with vengeance to defeat

Herding the congregation is a longsuffering task
Never hiding behind an earthly accepted mask
Standing with support and the love of his flock
He'll win souls from ole Satan's stock

Remembering purpose is his daily dare
His being was created with the Word to share
Intricate as the road may get from his life travels
Honors the challenge helping wayward souls unravel

Un-brokenness

Family circles are chained with God's grace
Never to be broken by the world's pace
A continuous evolution of all to come
Always knowing where the beginning is from

The circle of blood goes around and around
It is chained with celestial love to make it sound
Abound with strength from above
Strong, yet peaceful as a heavenly dove

A never-ending circle of generations to come
The supply of links is created from the great beyond
The circle's goodness keeps un-brokenness in existence
For the challenge is bound by family resistance

Evelyn Dilworth-Williams

Another Day

Morning comes with so many clouds in the sky
I rise with the wonder of how the day will pass by
A reality of the Herculean and poignant overcast
Clutches a stillness in my soul that seemingly last
The soberness of my mind is locked in dull unbelief
That the time from yesterday was no better relief
Still the folded morning challenges of life's way
Stake hold that the next coming is a better day

Inevitable Cycle

Just a lease
Birth is the seal
Creating its release
To forever reveal

When signed
Our stay begins
Making its kind
Still breathing ends

Temporary stay
On a parcel of earth
Though we pray
Termination activates at birth

Yet, ownership is claimed
Ne'er with control
Battling to tame
Mayhem takes hold

Possession is set
Peace with destruction
Co-existence unlikely met
Void of conception

Life's time is out
Though signed again
No doubt
With a lease

Evelyn Dilworth-Williams

Right Now

the joyous state
un-clouding the soul
revealing aptness
of changing time
with breathing roots
manning the stay
of life's power
appreciating self
as well as others
with or without
perfect harmony
with the remains
of energy awaiting
purposeful use
that stimulates
the dormant
essence being
to rejoice before
life creatures
as an example
of a natural treasure
possessed since birth
to timely share
with all as the
being's gift that
arrives and remains
with peaceful simplicity
and inward comfort
a blessed state
of rewarded bliss
that your time
presents

Exhale Life

Gently breathing to stroke earth
Exhaling to spring life forth
With brilliancy for all to see
Changing the old to new birth

Grandeur wonderment of life
Originating pauses for all in sight
With the lofty bustle of days about
A tender breath to ease life's bitter strife

Still I'm grasping from all around
From sufficient air to instill living needs
Awaiting the take hold of gifted control
Softly breathing with mightily audible sounds

What's there … With living pleasure and life's ease
Making a promise stay for all absorbing belief
Self-rendering inhales from morning 'til night
From the breath that supplies life's mainstay to please

The songs of morning again; a renewal of hope and gleaming efforts

My Daily Gift

What will I give today
To help someone along the way
Will I give a smile to a wayward child
Or a hand to a homeless man

What will I give today
To help someone along the way
For all that I give, I give with love

It's the gift given to me from heaven above
Will I share my earthly wealth
Or give a hand to others in failing health

What will I give today
To help someone along the way
For all that I give, I give with love

It's the gift given to me from heaven above
Shall I read a verse from the great Book
Or pray for someone with a troubled face look

What will I give today
To help someone along the way
For all that I give, I give with love

It's the gift given to me from heaven above
Will I speak words of kindness
And hope that even my enemy is blessed

What will I give today
To help someone along the way
For all that I give, I give with love

It's the gift given to me from heaven above
Shall I offer prayer
For the world's despair

What will I give today
To help someone along the way
For all that I give, I give with love

Chorus:
Whatever I give, I give with love,
Love given to me from heaven above
For it's the gift given to me today
So I'll share it with others along the way

Glory Be!

O' sunshine, sunshine glory be
what a wonderful day made for you
and me

O' sunshine, sunshine glory be
shine so bright that I may see

O' sunshine, sunshine glory be
warm my soul before I make my plea

O' sunshine, sunshine glory be
light my path so I can run free

O' sunshine, sunshine glory be
create newness for unworthiness like me

O' sunshine, sunshine glory be
hear my prayer while on bending knees

O' sunshine, sunshine glory be
praises to the Master for you and me

O' sunshine, sunshine glory be
O' sunshine, sunshine glory be

O' Sunshine, Sunshine Glory Be!

Along the Way

What can I do today
to help one of God's creatures along the way
Along the way, I'll help someone along the way

I'll smile at a wayward soul today
And comfort a down spirit, a spirit
That can't find words to pray

What can I do today
to help one of God's creatures along the way
Along the way, I'll help someone along the way

When in the shadows of grief
And a soul trembles without hope
All that I'll do will be for relief

What can I do today
to help one of God's creatures along the way
Along the way, I'll help someone along the way

When hatred of the helpless raises its head
And no hand reaches to stop it
I'll strive to conquer it before it spreads

What can I do today
to help one of God's creatures along the way
Along the way, I'll help someone along the way

About the Author

Evelyn Dilworth-Williams is a secondary teacher, guidance counselor, and a master facilitator of parenting education. She received her undergraduate degree from Miles College in Fairfield, Alabama and her graduate degree from the University of Alabama in Birmingham. AuthorHouse Publishers published her first selection of poems: Panola: My Kinfolks' Land in 2003. Her recent readings of her poetry have been at the Fifth Annual Summer Institute Family Research Consortium III in Santa Ana Pueblo, New Mexico, Afro-World in St. Louis Missouri, The Yo-Yo Sista's Book Club in North Carolina, Civil Rights Institute in Birmingham, the public libraries in Birmingham, Black History and Kwanzaa affairs, various heritage affairs, church and social gatherings.